The Parables for Today

also by A. M. Hunter

According to John
Design for Life
The Epistle to the Romans
The Fifth Evangelist
The Gospel According to St Mark
The Gospel According to St Paul
Interpreting the Parables
Introducing the New Testament
Jesus – Lord and Saviour
The Parables Then and Now
Preaching the New Testament
The Work and Words of Jesus

4.75

The Parables
for Today

A. M. HUNTER

SCM PRESS LTD

334 02236 3

First published in Britain 1983
by SCM Press Ltd
26–30 Tottenham Road, London N1

Typeset by Gloucester Typesetting Services
and printed in Great Britain by
Richard Clay (The Chaucer Press) Ltd
Bungay, Suffolk

CONTENTS

1

Introducing the Parables

What is a parable? The old definition, 'An earthly story with a heavenly meaning', can hardly be bettered. But the word itself, which is Greek in origin, means literally a 'comparison', as parable is a form of *teaching* which consists in comparing the unknown with the known, the strange with the familiar. It is matter of everyday experience that you cannot explain anything to somebody except by saying that it is 'like' something else. So Jesus' parables often begin, 'The kingdom of God is like' – like yeast, or a grain of wheat, or a costly pearl. Combine, then, this mode of teaching by analogy with the oriental's delight in pictorial speech and everyman's love of a story, and you have most of the reasons why men took to using parables in order to convey spiritual truth.

There are parables in the Old Testament like, for instance, Nathan's celebrated one to King David about the little ewe lamb (II Samuel 12.1–7); but the supreme master of parable was our Lord himself. The Gospels have preserved some sixty of his parables, some short, some long; and, thanks to modern scholars,[1] we may now understand them better than our forefathers did. Moreover, nowhere can we be surer that we are in touch with the Jesus of history than in his parables. First, because they mirror daily life in first-century Palestine as surely as William Cobbett's *Rural Rides* reflect country life in eighteenth-century England. Second, because, as we shall see, they reveal our Lord's highly original way of thinking and teaching. And, third, because great parables are evidently so hard to create that it is difficult to name another person in history with more than one or two good ones to his credit.

But here a caveat! It is a common mistake to regard Jesus' parables as just picturesque stories from which preachers may draw edifying 'morals' for today. 'Jesus told parables,' it has been well said, 'and Jesus was put to death.' Would men have crucified Jesus if he had just gone about Galilee and Judaea telling pleasant moralizing stories? Of course they would not! The truth is that Jesus' parables were more like Churchill's speeches in 1940 – weapons of war in a great campaign – the kingdom of God against the powers of evil which took Jesus finally to the Cross.

All Jesus' parables are, in one way or another, parables of the kingdom; that is, they have to do with the advent of the rule of God – God breaking into history in order to visit and redeem his people. For the burden of Jesus' Good News was that the reign of God, for which men had long hoped and prayed, was now beginning, and men must consider how to get into it (see Mark 1.14f. NEB: 'The kingdom of God is upon you').

Some parables, like The Sower and The Leaven tell of the coming and growth of God's kingdom. Others, like The Labourers in the Vineyard, describe the grace of the God who is now inaugurating his saving rule. Others, like The Hidden Treasure and The Precious Pearl, suggest what is required of candidates for the kingdom. Some, heavy with a sense of impending judgment, like The Man on the Way to Court and The Wicked Vinedressers, concern the crisis for Israel and the world created by Christ's ministry. Lastly, one or two parables look away to the great day when God will consummate his kingdom in glory and reward men according

2

to the good or evil they have done. Two such are the stories of The Last Judgment and Dives and Lazarus.

Here are five things to remember if you wish to interpret the parables rightly.

First, they are not fables (like Aesop's), but *stories from real life*: stories about baking and building, farming and fishing, weddings and funerals, warring kings and improvident bridesmaids, importunate widows and dishonest land-stewards, 'Holy Willies' and prodigal sons.

Next, Jesus used parables because 'truth embodied in a tale' is easy to remember (one might forget a sermon about the grace of God, but who that heard it could forget the story of The Prodigal Son?), and also because a parable, by its very nature, teases into thought and calls for a decision. Thus when Jesus ends a parable, as he often did, with the words 'He who has ears to hear, let him hear!', he means, 'This is more than just a pleasant or intriguing story. Ponder it well and work out its meaning for yourselves.' In other words, a parable is not a crutch for limping intellects but a spur to religious insight.

Third: Jesus' parables follow the rules of popular story-telling. One is the 'rule of contrast' whereby virtue and vice, wisdom and folly, riches and poverty are contrasted. Examples are The Wise and the Foolish Bridesmaids, The Two Builders, and Dives and Lazarus. Another is 'the rule of three' whereby the story has three characters. Recall the three travellers in the tale of The Good Samaritan or the three servants in that of The Talents. And a third is 'the rule of end-stress', whereby the spotlight falls on the last person or act in the series. Think of 'the lazy rascal' who did nothing with his talent, or the sending of the only son in the tale of The Wicked Vinedressers.

Fourth: a parable makes one point only, and the details in

3

the story are like the feathers which wing the arrow to its mark. In other words, we are not meant to seek for hidden meanings in details like the 'two pence' in the story of The Good Samaritan or 'the fatted calf' in that about The Prodigal Son, which would better be renamed 'The Waiting Father'.

Finally, remember that the parables form a running commentary on Jesus' ministry, first in Galilee and then in Judaea, and serve as prelude to the act which completed and crowned his whole mission. For there came a time when mere words were no longer of any avail, a time when only an act could effect what God had sent Jesus into the world to do. The Cross was, in fact, God's great parable acted out in history by which he sought to reconcile a prodigal human race to himself. This was what St Paul meant when he wrote to the Christians in Rome: 'God shows his love for us in that, while we were yet sinners, Christ died for us' (Rom. 5.8; cf. John 3.16).

Such are the main principles for interpreting the parables of Jesus. One word more, and that of capital importance for those who have to teach or preach the scriptures today. The parables are *works of art* which may be fruitfully applied to situations never contemplated at the time when they were first uttered. Thus that 'pearl among the parables', The Prodigal Son, which I have renamed 'The Waiting Father', may contain meanings and applications going beyond the narrator's original purpose. Accordingly, as 'Jesus Christ is the same yesterday, today and for ever' (Heb. 13.8), so his parables have a way of breaking the shackles of time and speaking their word of God to every age. In the ninth century, Matthias Claudius, Bishop of Turin, likened them to a fountain which never dries up. 'When you draw from this fountain of wisdom,' he wrote, 'it fills up again, and the second truth you derive is fuller and more splendid than the first.' Is not that still true today?

Those 'earthly stories with heavenly meanings', first spoken in Galilee and Judaea nearly twenty centuries ago, still carry their good news for modern man. They assure us that 'God's kingdom stands and grows for ever' – till it shall please him to wind up the scroll of history; they promise his forgiving grace for all penitent sinners; they tell us what kind of people God needs to do his work in the world today; and they confront us with the eternal issues which hang upon our decision when faced with God's challenge to us in his incarnate, crucified and risen Son.

2

Mustard Seed and Leaven

Luke 13.18–21

It is always hard, at the actual time, to know what is *going on* in what is *taking place*. This is true both in politics and religion. Take an example from British history. What took place at Runnymede in 1215 was that King John, much against his will, signed *Magna Carta*. This charter laid it down that no man could be punished without a fair trial. It also insisted that no new taxes should be imposed without the consent of the people's representatives. When King John reluctantly signed the document, few could have perceived what was really going on. Now, with the help of hindsight, we can see that what was being inaugurated was British Parliamentary democracy as we know it today.

So it was in the first century AD when Christ came into Galilee proclaiming: 'The time has come; the kingdom of God is upon you; repent and believe the good news' (Mark 1.14f. NEB). He was announcing that God's reign, his great saving intervention in history – for which men had long been praying – was now beginning.

If you and I had been among his hearers, I doubt if we would have guessed that a great turning-point in history had been reached. Only the man who made the announcement knew what was going on in what was taking place, knew that the living God was invading history 'for us men and for our salvation'.

So, in two short parables, Jesus gave his followers a hint of what God was doing.

The reign of God, he told them, is like what happens when a woman buries some yeast in half a hundredweight of flour. If you have ever seen a bit of yeast under a microscope, you will have some idea of what he meant. What happens is a small explosion, all bubbles and eruptions, which does not stop until the whole batch of flour is leavened.

Just so, says Christ, when God's reign enters history, it sets up a dynamic disturbance which no age or society can escape. Now God's great ferment is beginning, and go on it will till his kingdom triumphs over all evil.

Now consider that other parable about The Mustard Seed, in which Jesus told his hearers what was going on in what was taking place.

For long the mustard seed had been proverbial among the Jews for the smallest thing imaginable. 'Have you ever noticed,' asked Jesus, 'that everyday miracle which can transform a tiny seed into a shrub ten feet tall in which the birds of the air make their dwelling? Well, this miracle is about to happen in the spiritual world.'

'The birds of the air', i.e. the wild birds, was a Jewish nickname for the Gentiles; and ever since the time of the prophet Ezekiel (see Ezek. 17.22f.) the tree in whose branches the wild birds made their nests had been a symbol for a world-wide empire.

Just so, says Christ, the reign of God, which may now seem a thing of infinitesimal importance, is destined to span the earth and include in its sweep the Gentiles from afar.

Small beginnings, great endings – this is the point of these twin short parables.

What have they to say to us today?

Today there is no shortage of human sin and devilry in the world, so that even religious people sometimes tremble for the future of God's cause.

It is here that Christ's two parables ought to put courage and hope into the faint-hearted. In the mind of the Almighty, to whom 'a thousand years are as one day', is nineteen hundred years a long time? I once received a letter from the Queen, who had read a book of mine. (She is now the Queen Mother.) She began by confessing that she had read the last chapter, which was about Christ's resurrection, first. 'It was dreadful cheating, I know,' she wrote, 'but it makes a wonderful and hopeful background to the whole book, and I don't regret it. Perhaps the light of the Resurrection will yet flood the world.'

Oh if only our pessimists would read history with the Christian eyes of the Queen Mother! Nineteen hundred years have come and gone since the planting of the mustard seed and the putting-in of God's leaven; and we do not yet see the final issue of it all. But the church of Christ, which the dawning of God's kingdom brought into being, now numbers more than a thousand millions in the world. And still God's leaven is working among the sons of men, working often in ways unrecognized by us in all the turmoil of the times. Think of the revolt against un-Christian racism known as *apartheid*. Think of all that is meant by 'Christian Aid' and 'Christian Action'. Think of all those Pentecostal Christians who in the last decade or two have sprung up in the Americas and spread into Europe, with their new-found belief in the power of the Holy Spirit to defrost 'God's frozen people' and revive moribund churches.

Don't believe those prophets of doom who tell us that the church of Christ is dying. True, in our sick society in Britain today Christianity is under a cloud. But elsewhere in the world the sun is shining, the leaven is working, the seed sprouting. From Brazil in the West to New Guinea in the East the holy fire of the gospel spreads apace. In North Korea the growth of the church has been called 'incredible'. Even in Communist Russia, with its official atheism, the church is very much alive.

You fearful saints, fresh courage take! The divine ferment which began in Galilee goes on. The seed which God gave his Son to sow on earth still keeps growing.

If you want to see things in true historical perspective, visit that 3000-year-old yew tree in the churchyard at Fortingall in Perthshire, the reputed birthplace of Pontius Pilate who sent Jesus to the Cross – and (though he little guessed it) 'let him loose in the world where neither Roman nor Jew could stop his truth'. And, as you view that venerable yew tree, reflect that it was growing there one thousand years before the seed of God's kingdom had begun to germinate in Galilee.

So, lift up your hearts, you little-faiths! Only a small part of the scroll of history is yet unrolled. The new dawn which began in Galilee has yet greater splendours to unfold. As the late and great archbishop William Temple used to say, 'We are the early Christians', and we have God's great future – and hereafter – before us.

3

The Sower

Mark 4.3-8

When the Old Testament prophets spoke of the good time coming, they sometimes likened God to a great sower. So did Jesus in this parable. When and why did he tell this tale of the farmer and his varying fortunes?

Clearly it belongs to the open-air phase of his ministry in Galilee. As Saint Mark tells us, Jesus had begun his work in the towns, only to find that his good news about God's dawning kingdom fell on deaf or hostile ears. The Pharisees, who were the religious people of the day, didn't like it. No more did the Sadducees who were all for preserving the *status quo*. Jesus himself had been driven out of the synagogues. And even his own family appear to have had misgivings about him. Small wonder, then, that his Galilean followers began to be discouraged. Was the great emprise of God's dawning kingdom foredoomed to failure?

To such forebodings the story of The Sower was Christ's answer.

We may suppose that, as he was speaking to the crowds in Galilee, there appeared on a nearby hillside a farmer hand-casting his seed. Here was a picture from real life ready-made for his purpose. So he told the story of The Sower.

Some of the seed, said Jesus, fell upon the footpath running through the field, only for the hungry birds to swoop down and devour it. Some fell on ground where there was only a thin dusting of soil on top, with below it shelving rock. Up shot the young seeds; but when the sun pierced the shallow soil, the young plants quickly withered. Other seed fell on soil thick with thorns which shot up quickly and choked the growing corn-shoots. But this was not the end of the story. Some seed fell on good ground, and yielded the crop we all remember – 'some thirty, some sixty, and some a hundred fold'.

Kindly note the point of these percentages. In Palestine ten-fold was then reckoned a fair crop. In other words, the harvest in the story was a bumper one, a harvest fit to gladden any farmer's heart and make him forget his losses.

Now take a further point. The parables of Jesus generally follow the rules of popular story-telling. One of these is known as 'the rule of end-stress'. What this means is that the spotlight falls on the last item in the series – in this case, the abundant harvest.

Lift then the whole story from the natural to the spiritual world, and its meaning is clear. 'In spite of all losses,' Jesus is saying, 'the farmer reaps a splendid crop.' That is, God's kingdom advances and the harvest exceeds all expectations. As unproductive pockets of soil are every farmer's lot, so in history we must expect failures due to human sin and un-belief. But God's kingdom belongs to the eternal realm, and what matters is the bumper harvest, not the failures.

On our Lord's lips then the parable of The Sower is a *Nil desperandum!* – a ringing 'Have faith in God' – to his desponding followers. Nineteen centuries later, is it not still a clarion call to the 'fearful saints' among us?

Today, some Christians seem to be like the man who wrote the limerick:

God's Word made a perfect beginning:
Man spoiled the creation by sinning:
We know that the story
Will end in God's glory,
But at present the other side's winning.

Doesn't that poem describe how, in our black moods, we feel about God's cause in the world today? 'At present the other side's winning'?

What the parable of The Sower says to us is something like this: 'When you don't like the outlook, try the uplook.' In other words, the great Sower is very much alive, and active. Like a great wind, his holy Spirit is working in the world, so that the 'little flock' which the Good Shepherd gathered in Galilee long ago now numbers more than a thousand millions and, as statistics show, is gaining 55,000 converts every day, as every week 1400 new churches are established.[1]

'Ye fearful saints, fresh courage take!' The Lord God omnipotent reigneth, as his kingdom moves ever onward to its consummation. Lift up your hearts, you men of little faith! It is a vanquished world in which men play their devilries. God in Christ crucified and risen, has overcome it, and his final victory is assured:

For the Lord our God shall come
And shall take his harvest home;
From his field shall in that day
All offences purge away;
Give his angels charge at last
In the fire the tares to cast;
But the fruitful ears to store
In his garner evermore.

4

The Weeds among the Wheat

Matt. 13.24-30 NEB

'The corruption of the best,' says the proverb, 'is ever the worst.' There is a goodness which, paradoxically, can go bad. And how much harm can be done in the world by such 'good' people who do not know that they are not good!

People like the Pharisees in Christ's day. Their very name meant 'the Separatists'; their aim was a sort of spiritual *apartheid*; and we know from one of their writings that they expected a great separating of the sinners from the saints when it should please God to bring in his kingdom and send his Messiah.

But when Jesus the Messiah did come announcing the advent of God's reign, it seemed to the Pharisees that his followers included more sinners than saints. 'If the kingdom of God has really dawned,' we can almost hear them saying, 'why has there not been in Israel a weeding out of the sinners from the saints?'

For his answer Jesus told a story about a farmer who woke up one day to discover a lot of weeds among his wheat. The weed was darnel, and in the early stages of its growth only the expert eye can distinguish it from wheat.

'A man,' said Jesus, 'sowed his field with good seed; but while everyone was asleep, his enemy came, sowed darnel among his wheat, and made off.' (In the East, to this very day, men still play lousy tricks like this. Even in modern India the threat can still be heard, 'I will sow bad seed in your field.')

So the farmer's men went to their employer. 'Sir,' they said, 'was it not good seed that you sowed in your field? Then where has this wretched darnel come from?' 'This is an enemy's doing,' he replied. 'Then,' they asked, 'shall we go and gather up the darnel?' 'No,' he said, 'in gathering up the darnel you might pull up the wheat at the same time. Let them grow together until the harvest; and at harvest-time I will tell the reapers, Gather up the darnel and tie them in bundles for burning; then collect the wheat and store it in my barn.'

That is the story. Though he does not quote it, I think it may have been in St Paul's mind when he wrote his first letter to the Christians in Corinth. 'Pass no premature judgment,' he counselled them, 'wait till the Lord comes' (I Cor. 4.5 NEB).

Three centuries later, in North Africa, some strait-laced Christians, declaring that the church must be holy, called for the weeding-out of all sinners. The reply of their great bishop, Saint Augustine, was to point them to Christ's parable about the weeds among the wheat. He had rightly seen that it is a warning against premature weeding. No farmer in his senses, says Christ, tries to separate the weeds from the wheat while the crop is still growing. In plain terms, leave the weeding out of bad men from good to God at Judgment Day.

What then should our Lord's warning against premature weeding mean for us today?

We all know what a finicky business weeding can be, the dilemmas it presents to the gardener. Is this a weed, or is it a wild flower? How do you tell couch grass from good corn? And isn't the task still harder when we try to decide who are the saints and who the hell-deserving sinners?

You may remember the old rhyme:

> There is so much good in the worst of us,
> And so much bad in the best of us,
> That it hardly becomes any of us
> To talk about the rest of us.

Or, let me put it another way. Have you ever in your life met a person of whom you could say quite certainly, 'This man is a weed and nothing but a weed – a rotter to the very core, with no trace of God's image left in him?'

The truth is that, if the weeding out of the sinners from the saints were left to us fallible mortals, we would, as Jesus said, inevitably rip up much good wheat along with the weeds.

Did not Robert Burns have 'the mind of Christ' when he wrote:

> Who made the heart, 'tis He alone
> Decidedly can try us,
> He knows each chord, its various tone,
> Each spring, its various bias.

Not for us mortals, then, this task of sifting out sinners from saints! It is a task fit only for God, the great 'knower of hearts', at Judgment Day.

Such a Last Judgment the New Testament clearly teaches. Nowadays, however, we are told that 'modern man isn't bothering about his sins' and regards the Last Judgment as an outworn myth no longer credible by enlightened man. So, on the ultimate issues of life, he thinks himself wiser than Christ. But a true Christianity cannot dispense with the doctrine of man's final accountability to his maker for what he has done and been. This said, let it also be said that it is not for us to say who will finally stand on the Redeemer's right hand or his left, as Christ put it in his story about Judgment Day.

Nonetheless, we may dare to affirm three things, on the authority of Christ himself.

First, the Last Judgment will contain surprises, with some quite unexpected – and unexpecting – people gaining a heavenly reward; and, contrariwise, some expecting people in for rude shocks.

Second, the sentence of final exclusion from God's presence – which is what 'hell' means, and not eternal roasting in an oven – will not fall on any who do not freely and deliberately pronounce it upon themselves.

And, last, when Christ the King comes with his sickle and his crown, if there are surprises in store, one thing will be unchanged – the love which died on the Cross to save sinners, the love in which we have believed and hoped and endured.

Remembering these things, would not the best prayer for us all be just this:

> O may we stand before the Lamb
> When earth and seas have fled,
> And hear the Judge pronounce our name
> With blessings on our head.

5

Hidden Treasure and Precious Pearl

Matt. 13.44f.

In the spring of 1947 when two Arab lads were tending their sheep and goats at Qumran, near the north-west cliffs of the Dead Sea, one of their flock went missing. Searching for it, one lad threw a stone into a small cleft in the rock face. When he heard what sounded like breaking crockery, he took sudden fright. Later, the two lads crept together into the cave; and there on its floor, stuffed in long jars, behold, roll upon roll of crumbling leather! They had made one of the great archaeological discoveries of modern times. They had found what are called the Dead Sea Scrolls.

One day, some miles to the north, nineteen centuries earlier, Jesus, proclaiming the good news of God's dawning kingdom, told a similar story about the chance discovery of treasure trove. A farmer was ploughing a field when suddenly the coulter laid bare a cache of precious coins which, years before, someone had hidden to preserve it from advancing armies or marauding robbers. Making sure no one had seen him, he shovelled back the earth on the treasure and hurried home to scrape up every penny to buy that field.

On another occasion Jesus told a story about a trader whose business was the search for fine pearls. One day he had news of the sort of pearl he had been seeking for years – a pearl *par excellence*. Without more ado he sold all his assets and purchased that marvellous pearl.

These parables are twins, as the point of both is the same: 'How precious is a place in God's kingdom? Is not such blessedness worth any sacrifice?'

Yet between the two parables there is one difference. In The Hidden Treasure the man's wealth comes to him quite unexpectedly – like a godsend – whereas in The Precious Pearl the man finds it after long questing. Jesus is suggesting that it is often by very different roads that men enter into God's kingdom. Think, for example, of Matthew the tax-collector at Capernaum, busy levying tolls on passing merchandise for his Roman overlords, when Jesus, on his way through town, cries, 'Follow me!' and Matthew rises up and absconds from his desk, to follow the Messiah. Is not Matthew like the man who found the hid treasure all un-expectedly? How different it was to be for Paul! His road began in distant Tarsus, wound round the rabbinical aca-demy of Gamaliel in Jerusalem and ended – only to begin wonderfully again – on the road to Damascus.

There were many ways then, as there still are today, into God's kingdom and faith in Christ who is its embodiment. Some find the way at revivalist meetings; others, like Blaise Pascal, the great French scientist, in a soul-shaking experience of spiritual 'fire'; and others again, like the Oxford don, C. S. Lewis, after long questioning, on a sunny morning, driving down to Whipsnade. 'When we set out,' he wrote, 'I did not believe that Jesus Christ was the Son of God. When we reached the zoo, I did.'

In all this we have been speaking of Christ the Son of man (as he called himself) and the kingdom of God as though they were separate and unrelated, he the proclaimer of the kingdom and the kingdom itself the reign of God his Father. But you cannot study the Gospels carefully without perceiving that to follow Christ is to be *in* the kingdom; that it is where he is; that, in short, the kingdom of God is Christ himself. As Karl Barth, greatest of modern theologians, put it, 'Jesus spoke of the kingdom of God and he *was* the kingdom of God.' This is why, after the miracle of the first Easter Day, the apostles preached Christ rather than the kingdom. The gospel of the kingdom was Christ in essence; the risen Christ was the gospel of the kingdom in power. He was the truth of his own great gospel. It is wherever he is, and to confess him as your Saviour and Lord is to ensure it, to have eternal life.

For proof of this read the third chapter of Paul's letter to the Philippians. There the apostle tells us how, like the trader in the parable, he surrendered everything he held dear – all his proud privileges as a Jew – in order to gain the pearl of the kingdom which was Christ, that Christ in whom, as he said, were 'unfathomable riches' (Eph. 3.8), in whom 'were hidden all God's treasures of wisdom and knowledge' (Col. 2.3).

Now, finally, come down to the twentieth century and ourselves.

Our world contains various religions, with doubtless a grain of God's truth in each of them, since, in all generations, as Paul said, God has not left himself some witness – 'some clue to his nature' (Acts 14.17 NEB). But, when the chips are really down – when it isn't an armchair argument or a debating society but the matter of a faith to live by in this world – what else is there, who else is there, but that Christ in whom the apostles and countless Christians down the centuries have found God's hidden treasure and precious pearl embodied in a man?

Here in Christ, incarnate, crucified, risen, exalted, and now, through the Holy Spirit, present with his people, is all that the religious heart of man could desire – the assurance, through the Cross, of God's forgiveness for his sin, the promise and power of new beginnings, and a kingdom which calls him to service among his fellow men, and which is invincible and everlasting.

Is not this spiritual wealth which demonetizes all other currencies? Is not this heavenly treasure which will last on when all the ephemeral prizes on which wordlings set their hearts pass and perish? So wrote that 'prophet for today', P. T. Forsyth, in his great book *The Person and Place of Jesus Christ*:

> I should count a life well spent and a world well lost if, after tasting all its experiences and facing all its problems, I had no more to show at its close, or carry with me into another world, than the acquisition of a real, sure, humble and grateful faith in the eternal and incarnate Son of God.

And to all in our world who have lost their spiritual bearings this Christ still comes, offering them the treasure and the pearl which carry with them the promise of eternal life. Still, as of old in Galilee, comes his challenge: 'Follow me! I am the true and living Way to God. No one comes to the Father but by me. Is not such blessedness worth any sacrifice? If I offer you a cross, I also offer you a crown. If I offer you struggle, there will also be victory. Look life in the face. Look death in the face. Sum it all up, and make your decision!'

6

The Great Supper

Luke 14.15–24

When pious Jews in Christ's day thought about the coming time of salvation, they commonly pictured it as a great banquet. Thus did the Pharisee who, sitting one day at table with Jesus, said to him, 'How happy will the man be who sits down to feast in the kingdom of God!'

Jesus was never taken in by men who made merely pious noises. He had his own way of bringing them down to earth by the shortest possible route, as he now did. The pious man's unspoken thought was, 'When the roll is called up yonder I'll be there.' So Jesus told him a story.

There was once a host, he said, who prepared a great supper to which he had previously invited various guests. When the day came and 'all things were ready', he sent out a servant to remind the guests of his invitation. But the guests suddenly found that they had more important things to do, and one after another they replied, 'Sorry, I cannot come. Please accept my apologies.'

Predictably, the host 'was not amused'. Resolved to fill all the places at his table, he now sent his servant forth on a new search, first for the waifs and strays in the streets and alleys (which suggests the publicans and sinners) and then, when there was still room, for the vagrants in the highways and hedges (which suggests the Gentiles). 'Constrain them to come in,' he instructed his servant, 'for I want my house to be full.'

That is the story. What Jesus was saying to his pious friend was something like this: 'You think God's kingdom is a future prospect to be contemplated with unctuous anticipation. You are wrong. It is a present and blessed reality, calling for your response now. But what have you Pharisees done? You have declined God's invitation to his supper, and now he is offering its blessings to all his lost and despised children.'

Jesus spoke this parable to the churchmen in Israel, the professedly religious in the land. But it still carries a message for us today.

'When thou hadst overcome the sharpness of death,' says the *Te Deum*, 'thou didst open the kingdom of heaven to all believers.' That is to say, the blessings of God's kingdom are now open to all men of faith, whatever their race or colour. But, as in Christ's day, when confronted with his call into God's kingdom, men often reply: 'I have more important things to do. I cannot come. Please make my apologies.' And their excuses are basically the same.

'I am in the act of buying an estate,' said the first man in the story, 'and I must inspect it before completing the purchase.' For 'estate' write 'investments', and you have a modern equivalent. How many are so preoccupied with increasing their material possessions that they have no time to hear the still small voice of God! In Bernard Shaw's play *Saint Joan* we hear a conversation between the Maid and the Dauphin, the French king's eldest son. Joan heard voices from God telling her what to do. The Dauphin was exasperated. 'Oh your voices, your voices,' he said, 'Why don't the voices come to me? I am king and not you.' And the Maid answered, 'They do come, but you don't hear them.' Are not some of us today like the Dauphin? 'The world is too much with us, late and soon,' for us to hear and obey the voice of God.

'I am in the act of buying five yoke of oxen,' said the second man in the story, 'and I must try them out before I buy.' Nowadays the same man's excuse might be, 'I have bought a new car and it needs cleaning and polishing.' So, on Sunday mornings, instead of going to church as his fore-fathers did, he bows down before his brazen idol, whether it be a Mini Metro or a Mercedes.

'I have just married a wife,' said the third man in the story, 'and therefore I cannot come.' The 'wife' stands for the new bliss of marriage and a home of one's own. Now, as Robert Burns phrased it,

> To make a happy fireside clime
>   To weans and wife,
> That's the true pathos and sublime
>   Of human life.

Nonetheless, it is one of the tragedies of life when good things like these are allowed to shut out the claims of that God who 'has made us for himself'.

Worldly possessions, business preoccupations, domestic ties, are still the things which can make men deaf to the claims of God's kingdom. So easy is it for us to become so absorbed in the things of time that we forget the things which are unseen and eternal.

A Danish fable tells how a spider once slid down a filament of thread from the rafters of the barn and established himself upon a lower level. There he spread his web, caught plenty of flies, and grew sleek and prosperous. One day however, wandering about his premises, he saw the thread which stretched up into the unseen above him. 'What is that for?'

said the spider, and snapped it. And all his little house of life collapsed. Need the moral be drawn?

From the three excuse-makers now come back again to the main story. One point clearly made is that nobody is excluded from God's kingdom except by his own choice. But the parable is also saying, if we hear it properly, 'Now is the accepted time!' The pious man said, 'How happy will he be who sits down hereafter at God's great banquet!' Our Lord's reply was: 'If a man does not here and now accept God's invitation, it may be too late.'

Still today, through Christ, God's invitation into his kingdom goes out; and even now we are all writing our replies. Either it is, 'Please make my apologies,' which is only another way of saying, 'I have more important things to do.' Or else it is, 'I know my heart's deepest need. I am weary of my sins and need forgiveness. Lord God, you have offered it to us in Christ your Son who died upon the Cross to reconcile sinners to yourself, and with all my heart I accept it.'

7

The Waiting Father

Luke 15.11–32

The parable of The Prodigal Son is the most famous short story every told. Why did Jesus tell it? To whom was it addressed? And is the traditional name for it the right one? These are our questions.

The only explanation which makes sense of this story is that the Father represents God, the elder brother the Pharisees who had criticized Jesus for opening God's kingdom to outcasts and sinners, and the younger brother those very sinners whom Jesus went out of his way to befriend.

In the parable, therefore, God, by the lips of Jesus, declares his free forgiveness for penitent sinners, while at the same time gently rebuking the Pharisees, who were 'the Holy Willies' of their day.

Now, if this is true, the traditional title for the parable – The Prodigal Son – won't do. Some have proposed to rename it 'The Two Lost Sons'. There is some force in this, for, if the younger son was 'lost' in 'the far country', the elder son was no less 'lost' at home, behind a barricade of self-righteousness.

Yet even this title gets the parable out of focus; for the chief character in it is neither of the two sons but the father. Right up to the very last scene he broods over the whole story. Therefore the only proper title for the story is 'The

Waiting Father' – the father who waits because he loves, the father who represents God.

This is the first point to seize. Now take a further step. Jesus' parables, as we have seen, are all stories from real life. To this rule our parable seems no exception. They had prodigal sons in Jesus' day, as we still have them – those young men (and women) who say, 'Why can't I get away for a while from parental control – the old man (or the old woman) is getting on my nerves?' In the same way every generation has its 'far country', and one of its names today is 'Hippie Land'.

Yet, if this is a story from real life, it is something more. Many have taken Jesus to be saying in it, 'This is how an earthly father would treat his returning prodigal, and will not the good Father above?' But question: Is this in fact how earthly fathers always welcome home their returning prodigals? Do they really run to kiss them, load them with new clothes and expensive presents, and reward them with a barbecue and a ball?

You may have heard the story of the modern prodigal son who, on turning up in the 'far country' of a neighbouring parish, was advised by the local minister to 'go back home and his father would kill the fatted calf for him'. The prodigal did so and, months later, meeting the minister again, was asked hopefully, 'Well, and did your father kill the fatted calf for you?' 'No,' came the rueful reply, 'but he nearly killed the prodigal son!' Who will deny that it often happens so, even in this 'permissive society' of ours?

The point is that Jesus' story is here larger than life. The father of the prodigal is not an ordinary human father but, as we say in Scotland, a 'byordinar' one. What Jesus is here describing is the extravagant love of God – his sheer grace – to undeserving men.

What then has the parable to say to us? How shall we apply it to our human situation today?

First, let the younger son stand for all those young men and women who, fed up with 'the Establishment', rebel against law and order in every shape and form. Likewise, let the elder son stand for all the unadventurous, conventional Christians who turn a cold, disliking eye on their rebellious contemporaries.

To those stay-at-home Christians – those 'dull prissy paragons', as the prodigals might call them – who complain that they have always done what they should but have never had any 'bright lights' in their lives, the father in the story is saying, 'Son, you are always with me, and all that is mine is yours.' In other words, if you are in the elder brother's shoes, thank God for all the blessings you so lightly take for granted, and be grateful you have escaped all the heartache and hopelessness of your contemporaries. And to the modern prodigals, the father, who is God, is saying, 'You chose freedom, and I didn't stop you. All the time you have been in the far country, I have been worrying about you. And here I am, still waiting to welcome you home.'

For the abiding truth of this parable is that behind the drift of human things, and brooding over them in compassion, is an almighty Father, and that, as St Augustine, himself the greatest returned prodigal of them all, put it: 'Our hearts will never be at rest until they find rest in him.'

In other words, there can be a homecoming for us all, because there is a home. The door of the kingdom, which leads to our Father's house with its 'many rooms', still stands open, as there is one who has died and risen to open it, and who still says to us today, 'I am the true and living way to the Father.'

The decisive question for each one of us is: do we want to come home? 'Behold I stand at the door and knock,' says

Christ, 'If anyone hears my voice and opens the door, I will come in to him, and eat with him, and he with me. He who conquers, I will grant him to sit with me on my throne, as I myself conquered and sat down with my Father on his throne. He who has an ear to hear, let him hear!' (Rev. 9.20ff.).

8

The Kind Employer

Matt. 20.1–15

The story of the labourers in the vineyard reminds us of our old 'Feeing Fairs' when farmworkers, seeking employment, would meet their prospective employers. A bargain would be struck, conditions agreed, and a wage fixed. But, though the setting of Christ's story is the market-place, which was the employment exchange of the day, is it, as some have supposed, a story about 'the just wage'?

The short answer is: the grumblers in the story are the Pharisees, those goody-goody Jews who complained that Jesus was opening the gates of God's kingdom to all sorts of dubious characters known as tax-gatherers and sinners, and the parable is a story about the grace of God.

But to the tale. It was autumn in Palestine and time to gather in the grape harvest. Since the rainy season was near, speed was of the essence, with the more hands the better. So, one morning, at 6 a.m., the owner of the estate (whom we will call 'the employer') set out to engage harvesters. Finding some, he agreed to pay them a pound a day, and the first squad started work. About 9 a.m., coming on some idle men in the market-place, the employer bade them join the first lot, promising them a 'fair wage'. So they too started work. At noon, and again at 3 p.m., he did likewise. Then, about 5 p.m., meeting some more unemployed, he said, 'Go

29

and join the others in my vineyard.'

But the really surprising thing happened about one hour later when falling darkness put an end to labour. Jewish law laid it down, 'You shall not keep back a hired man's wages till next morning.' So the employer said to his manager, 'Call the workers together and pay them their wages, beginning with the last arrivals and ending with the first.'

When the last-comers stepped forward, though all they were entitled to was about eight pence, each got a pound in his hand, that is, a full day's wage. But, looking on, were the first-comers who had begun work at daybreak; and when they saw what the late-comers got, and then themselves received the same amount, they were not amused. 'These layabouts,' they protested, 'have worked only one hour, and yet you have put them on the same level as us who have been sweating it out in the heat of the sun since dawn. Is this what you call justice?'

It is the kind of protest that any good trade-unionist would make today. 'Look, friend,' said the employer to the chief protester, 'I am not cheating you. Did we not agree on a pound a day? Well, you have got it. Off with you! If it is my pleasure to pay the last-comers the same as you, am I not free to do as I will with what is my own? Or are you jealous because I am generous?'

So we come back to the question, 'Was Jesus really discussing the problem of what nowadays we call "the just wage"?'

He was not. He was answering those goody-goody Jews, the Pharisees, who imagined that their piety entitled them to a special claim on God's reward and were shocked to see Jesus admitting all those 'bad characters' into his Father's kingdom. For the crux of the whole story comes with that settlement at sunset and the astonishing generosity of the employer to the late-comers, i.e. the tax-gatherers and sinners.

This, then, is not the story of The Labourers in the Vine-yard, as tradition has named it. It is the story of The Kind Employer. He is the chief character in the story, and he represents God.

In his story Jesus is not talking about equal pay for equal work. He is talking theology, not economics. 'The rewards of God's kingdom,' he is saying, 'are measured not by men's deserts but by their needs. God treats sinners as that kind employer treated those unemployed men. This is what the heavenly Father is like; and, because he is like this, and acts like this, so do I.'

The parable, then, is not about 'the just wage'. It is about the grace of God. But, someone may say, what relevance has it for us? Are not those Pharisees to whom Christ told it long dead and buried? Dead they may be, but have they not from time to time down the Christian centuries had their spiritual successors? Have we forgotten how many pious Christians criticized John Wesley for taking the gospel to the 'sinners' of his day – those colliers, weavers and day-labourers whom he won for Christ? Or have we forgotten how last century many pious Christians sneered at William Booth for offering 'soup, soap and salvation' to the East-enders of London? Does not every generation produce its unlovely crop of self-righteous Christians who would fain make a 'closed shop' of God's kingdom and try to exclude all who do not measure up to their standards?

The story of The Kind Employer makes certain things quite clear.

It reminds us all how fortunate it is that God does not deal with us on the basis of strict justice. Was not this Portia's plea to the Jew Shylock in *The Merchant of Venice*?

Though justice be thy plea, consider this:
That in the course of justice none of us
Should see salvation. We do pray for mercy.

Christ's parable reminds us that God's thoughts are not our thoughts, nor his ways our ways (Isa. 55.8), for 'the love of God is broader than the measure of man's mind'.

Moreover, it tells us that there is an equal reward for all in his Father's kingdom. Does this shock us? An equal reward for the poorest and least worthy of Christ's followers along with great Christians like Paul and Augustine, Francis and Luther, Wesley and Livingstone, Dietrich Bonhoeffer and Maximilian Kolbe the saint of Auschwitz, Mary Slessor of Calabar and Mother Teresa of Calcutta? It doesn't make sense, and it doesn't sound fair; but it is the will of God, and it is very wonderful. This, says our Lord to us, is what God is like. And if he is like this, how dare we be jealous? On the contrary, is not Christ saying to us in this story what he says to us more plainly in his Sermon on the Mount, 'There must be no limit to your goodness, as your heavenly Father's goodness knows no bounds'?

9

The Good Samaritan

Luke 10.25-37

Some men revel in an argument about religion and love to score a point at an opponent's expense. But sometimes 'the worm turns' and (to mix our metaphors) the contentious man finds himself 'hoist with his own petard'.

Once during his ministry, St Luke tells us, our Lord himself had been the target for cross-examination by a 'lawyer'. By a 'lawyer' St Luke means an expert in the Law of Moses – the Ten Commandments and the hundreds of rules and regulations that had been added to them by the Scribes who were the theologians of the day. In order to understand the encounter between the lawyer and our Lord, we need to remember that, before this, Jewish theologians had summed up the Law in two verses from the Old Testament: (*a*) Deut. 6.5: 'You shall love the Lord your God with all your heart'; and (*b*) Lev. 19.18: 'You shall love your neighbour as yourself.'

Moreover, remember that the Jews regarded the word 'neighbour' as a term of limited liability. Not for one moment would they admit that it included dogs of Gentiles or half-breed heretics like the Samaritans.

When therefore the lawyer put his question to Jesus: 'Master, what must I do to inherit eternal life?', it was not because he wished to know the answer – he knew it already –

but because he wished to cross-examine our Lord as an authority on the sacred Law. Little did the examiner guess how he himself was about to be examined!

Jesus said to him, 'What is the Law's answer to this question of yours?' Replied the lawyer, 'Thou shalt love the Lord thy God with all thy heart, and thy neighbour as thyself.'

'Right answer,' replied Jesus, 'Do this, and you are on road to eternal life.'

It was then that the lawyer felt emboldened to put the question he was really spoiling to ask. 'And who, pray, is my neighbour?' 'Where do I draw the line?'

The lawyer wanted a theological argy-bargy. Jesus declined his invitation. Instead, he told a story not to answer the lawyer's question but to show him that his was the wrong question. The right question is not 'Whom may I consider my neighbour?' It is: 'To whom can I *be* a neighbour?' And the right answer to this is: 'Any human being who stands in need of my help.'

Now to the story. First, we see the lone traveller making his way along the so-called 'Path of Blood', those seventeen miles of dangerous road that slope down from Jerusalem to Jericho. Suddenly the robbers swoop, beat up their man, strip him of his valuables, and vanish as quickly as they came. A little later, along come two pillars of the Jewish church – a priest and one of the minor clergy, a Levite. They can't help seeing the wounded man, but not a finger do they lift to help him. We are not told why. Perhaps they feared that the robbers might reappear and clobber them too. Or maybe they feared that, if they stayed to help, they would be late for their sacred duties in the Temple. What we do know is that, human nature being what it is, we often find reasons for evading a distasteful duty. So off go priest and Levite

34

on their famous wide detour: 'they passed by on the other side'.

Then along comes the hero of the story, and of all persons he is a Samaritan – a half-breed heretic with whom no orthodox or self-respecting Jew would have anything to do, for 'the Jews have no dealings with the Samaritans' (John 4.9).

One look at the victim is enough. Dismounting, the Samaritan applies first aid, wine and oil to disinfect the wounds, and bandages to bind them up. Then, hoisting the man on his own beast, he makes for the nearest hostelry to care for him that night. Next morning he produces what in our money would be at least two 'fivers'. 'Look after him,' he says to the hotel-keeper, 'and if you have to spend any more on him, I will reimburse you on the way back.'

The story told, Jesus asks the final question: 'Which of these three men proved neighbour to the man who fell among the robbers?' The lawyer returns the only possible answer, 'Why the man who showed kindness to him.' 'Then,' said Jesus, 'Go and do as he did.'

With the exception of The Prodigal Son, no story Jesus told has so left its mark on our language and life. Today we even have a body of selfless people called 'The Telephone Samaritans', dedicated to helping people in dire distress of body or mind. But have we fully understood the meaning of the story? Am I wrong in supposing that we usually think of it as the story of the man who did his good deed?

Yet isn't the real point of the story this, that one's neighbour may well be the man we least expect? 'How can I love my neighbour when I don't know who he is?', said the lawyer. 'Real love never asks questions like this,' says Jesus. 'It knows no bounds of race. All it asks for is opportunities of going into action.'

35

Who is my neighbour? To that question our Lord still answers, 'Wrong question! The right question is, To whom can I be a neighbour?' But he doesn't stop there, to all of us who call ourselves his followers he is saying, 'Forget about creed or colour. Go and do what that Samaritan did, to all unfortunates who meet you on life's Path of Blood.'

One word more. We know that in the early church scholars identified the Good Samaritan with Christ himself. Nowadays, with our better understanding of his parables, somebody may object: 'This is bad exegesis, or interpretation. A parable is not an allegory. To identify Christ with the Good Samaritan is to allegorize the parable, and that is wrong.' Fair enough! But, if this old interpretation isn't exegetically right, isn't it evangelically true? For did not the teller of the parable himself become the Good Samaritan of our race when, by his Cross, he found healing for our stripes and forgiveness for our sins?

If this is true, and it is the heart of the gospel, are not you and I under obligation to honour and serve the hidden Christ who confronts us, as he tells us in his parable of The Last Judgment, in all his needy and stricken brothers?

If you visit the Holy Land today, your guide may point out to you 'The Inn of the Good Samaritan' on the Jericho Road. But the Jericho Road is not now in Israel only – like the living Christ, it is everywhere. For you and me it might be the London Road or the Glasgow Road. Sooner or later you and I find ourselves on it, confronted by a stricken or needy brother or sister. And to us, as to that lawyer long ago, comes our Lord's command, 'Go, and do as he did!'

10

The Pharisee and the Publican

Luke 18.9–14

Real holiness when you find it in man or woman – be it a Francis of Assisi or a Mother Teresa of Calcutta – is a beautiful and godlike quality. But when holiness turns to 'holier-than-thou-ness', the best becomes the worst, and holy ones become 'Holy Willies', like the one in Burns's poem.

Study the New Testament, and you will see that both our Lord and St Paul agree that none are so far from God as the self-righteous. For when a man knows that he is righteous, the odds are that he is not. Dr Spurgeon, the famous preacher, once said that he thought a certain man in his congregation the holiest he had ever known – till the man told him so himself!

It was to rebuke those who were 'sure of their own goodness' that Jesus told the story of The Pharisee and the Publican.

The Pharisees were the ultra pious people in Israel, or thought themselves such. The trouble was that in many cases their religion had gone bad on them. The best had become the worst, so that they held aloof from the common people who did not observe all the Ten Commandments or all the Mosaic rules and regulations.

Among these they included the 'publicans', or tax-collectors. These were the men who ingathered the imperial taxes for their Roman overlords and made a handsome 'cut' for themselves in so doing. In short, every right-thinking Pharisee regarded them as rogues and renegades.

But the Pharisee and the Publican, or tax-collector, are really timeless characters. Every age produces them, and we might even catch an occasional glimpse of them in the mirror!

Look first at the contrast between the two men. Try to picture the Pharisee swaggering up the Temple steps into the divine presence. He glowers at the tax-collector – what right has that wretch to be here at all? And then 'taking up his stance by himself' – aloof from the common herd – he pours the tale of his own righteousness into the ear of God.

How differently the tax-collector goes into the presence of God! He stands 'afar off', with his eyes fixed not on heaven but on earth, and he keeps beating his breast, overwhelmed by the sense of his own distance from God. Not a word has he to say in criticism of his neighbours – only seven short words which echo Psalm 51: 'God, be merciful to me a sinner!' Yet these seven words reveal the whole man as on a dark night a flash of sheet lightning will reveal a whole landscape.

Now contrast the prayers of the two men. The Pharisee's prayer is really a catalogue of negative virtues plus what theologians call 'works of supererogation' – that is, extra acts of piety calculated to establish a man's claim upon God's favour.

He begins by thanking God that he is not like other men – robbers, swindlers, adulterers – or, for that matter, like the tax-collector. Then he proceeds to rehearse his extra merits in the Almighty's ear. Twice a week, on Mondays and Thursdays, he fasts. But, besides fasting, he gives God ten per cent of all he gets. Probably he told God a good deal more about himself; for the whole burden of his prayer is himself, and pulsating through it you can hear that horrid little pronoun 'I'.

Very different is the tax-collector's prayer. No question of merits in his case. He has seen his own sinfulness against the burning holiness of God, and all he can blurt out is, 'God, be merciful to me a sinner!' Someone has said that when the heart is stirred, it speaks in telegrams. The tax-collector's prayer is like that.

You can tell a man's character from the books he reads or the friends he keeps. But, if you could hear them, nothing would reveal a man more than his prayers. The Pharisee comes out in his – his snobbery, his sanctimony, his mawkish self-esteem. Mind you, the things of which he boasts are not bad things. He goes to synagogue on Saturdays. He gives ten per cent of his income for religious purposes. His private life is possibly above suspicion. The trouble is that he knows his own goodness. The good man has become what the Scots call 'unco guid'.

It would be wrong to whitewash the tax-collector. He has faults aplenty. He lives by what we call 'graft'. By patriotic standards he is a traitor. Doubtless his private life contains some guilty secrets. But he knows it – knows that he is a sinner, that the holy God hates sin, and he casts himself on the Everlasting Mercy, imploring only forgiveness.

> Two men went up to pray. O rather say,
> One went to brag – the other went to pray.

Look last of all at the answers which the two prayers received. What nowadays we call 'the punch line' comes in the last sentence of the story. 'It was this man, the tax-collector', said Jesus, 'and not the other, who went home acquitted of his sins.' The tax-collector was accepted and forgiven by God; the Pharisee was not. In fact, his prayer did him harm. The man who is as good as he wishes to be will get worse, not better. This was the Pharisee's condition. His prayer was not heard.

George Meredith once wrote:

Who rises from his prayer a better man
His prayer is answered.

The tax-collector's prayer was answered. He rose 'a better man', not because he had been transformed into a spotless saint but because he knew that God had forgiven his sins.

'When the tax-collector prayed, "God, be merciful to me a sinner",' said the Danish philosopher Kierkegaard, 'it showed his awareness of being in danger.' And it not this the Word of God that Jesus still speaks to us through the parable?' The Pharisees may long be dust, but 'their soul goes marching on' – even in church. What we call 'Pharisaism' is still with us. We still tend to reproduce in our acts and attitudes that unlovely self-righteousness which Jesus pilloried in his parable. We show little awareness of the 'danger' referred to by Kierkegaard. And that goes not only for the ultra pious who are quite sure they are 'saved', but for all church people who are at ease in their own little Zions. May God, in his mercy, jolt us all out of our spiritual self-complacency!

11

The Two Debtors

Luke 7.36–50

How much harm is done in the world, and to the Christian cause, by 'good' people who do not know that they are not 'good' – people like Simon the Pharisee in St Luke's story or William Fisher of Mauchline, the original of 'Holy Willie' in Burns's poem! Even today the breed is not yet extinct, and they do not a little to keep some of our young folk from becoming members of Christ's church.

But to our story. Here was a pious and prosperous Jewish churchman named Simon. Curious to know more, at first hand, about this extraordinary man from Nazareth, he had invited him to dinner. While the meal was in progress, suddenly into his dining-room there came, uninvited, a well-known prostitute, carrying an alabaster bottle of perfume, and making a bee-line for Simon's distinguished guest.

But before she could get the stopper out of her bottle her tears were falling on Jesus' feet as he reclined at the table. Then, quite disgracefully, she was letting her hair down to wipe her tears away (though no respectable woman would do a thing like this in the presence of men), while she covered Jesus' feet with her kisses and poured her precious perfume over them.

Imagine if you can the look of horror on Simon's face, horror at his guest's acceptance of her homage.

What lay behind this astonishing display of devotion to Jesus? There can be but one explanation. Jesus had encountered the woman before and, by his assurance to her of God's forgiveness for her sins, had brought her to a true repentance.

But poor, prudish, pious Simon cannot see it this way. All he can see is the sort of woman who has invaded his privacy. All he can mutter is, 'If this man Jesus were really a prophet, he would have known what kind of woman was touching him.'

'Simon,' said Jesus, reading his thoughts, 'I have something to say to you.'

'Once there were two debtors. One owed his creditor fifty pounds, the other five. When they had nothing to pay with, the money-lender let them both off.'

Here note what a quite unheard-of creditor this is. No human money-lender in his senses thus lets off his debtors. Jesus is thinking of the great creditor above, to whom you and I pray, 'Forgive us our debts (i.e. our sins) as we also have forgiven our debtors (those who have sinned against us).' 'Can't you see, Simon,' Jesus is saying, 'that this poor woman is showing her gratitude to God for the forgiveness of her sins?'

But Simon remains blissfully unaware that the parable is directed at himself. 'You ask me,' he replies, 'which of the two debtors will be more grateful to his creditor? Why, of course the one who was let off more.'

'Right answer,' replies Jesus. Then: 'Simon, my friend, do you see this woman?' It was not a casual question. 'This woman' was precisely what Simon could not see. All he could see was the sort of woman she was – a trollop, a harlot, a loose woman of the streets.

So Jesus must strike the blindness from Simon's soul. 'When I came into your dining-room, Simon,' he says, 'you gave me no kiss of welcome. This woman has never ceased kissing my feet. You gave me no basin of water to wash them. This woman has washed them with her tears. You gave me no oil for my head. This woman has anointed my feet with her precious perfume.'

For Jesus, these little oriental courtesies – kiss, water and oil – were not trivial. They revealed the woman as Simon's omission of them revealed the Pharisee.

Though Simon was far from 'good' in God's sight, he showed no sense of his own sinfulness; but sin, sin incarnate and unashamed, he could see in the woman. For her part, the woman could only express her overwhelming debt to Jesus for mediating to her God's forgiveness.

'And so I tell you,' concluded Jesus, 'her great love proves that God has forgiven her her many sins.'

Does not this gospel story still rebuke the Pharisee lurking still in many a Christian soul, your soul and mine? We can all see and condemn wickedness in other people. But if many of us were as really concerned with the reformation of sinners as we profess to be, should we not begin with what Carlyle called 'the blackguard under our own bonnets'? The contemplation of human sin and folly with the aid of a looking-glass, it has been well said, is a less congenial occupation, but can be very salutary!

Come back again to Jesus' question to the Pharisee: 'Simon, do you see this woman?' No casual question this, but one that went to the very heart of the matter. Simon liked to arrange people in classes, and for him this woman's class was 'sinner', with a capital S. And, having established her class, he knew how she should be treated. Our Lord never classified people this way. He was not interested in the class to which they belonged, but in who they really were. He was concerned with them as persons: nay more, as potential sons and daughters in God's family and future dwellers in his 'Father's House' on high. And the clear implication of this story is that some whom we may account hell-deserving sinners may in fact be nearer to God than some 'unco guid' church members.

It makes us think, or ought to. How do you see and treat people? As 'sorts of persons' to be classified and condemned, or as real persons. precious to God, to be pitied and helped and saved?

Surely, as we profess to follow Christ, the right answer is not in doubt, and our Christian duty plain.

12

The Rascally Factor[1]
Luke 16.1–8 NEB

There was once a wealthy laird who had a dishonest factor. When somebody whispered to the laird that the factor was feathering his own nest out of the estate, the laird summoned him and faced him with his misdeeds. 'You had better turn in your accounts,' he told him, 'for I mean to sack you.'

The factor wasted no time cursing the laird or those who had 'split' on him. He said to himself, 'I am going to get my books any day now. But what am I to do after I get them? I am too soft for manual labour, and I am too proud to live on charity. But wait! Even if I am going to be without a job, I think I can see a way of keeping in with my friends.

So, without more ado, he sent word to the chief farmers who had loans from the estate. 'Come and see me at my office,' he said.

When the first farmer appeared, the factor asked him, 'What is your debt to the laird?' 'One thousand gallons of oil,' was the answer. 'Very well,' said the factor, 'You've got the bill I sent you? Take it and change the ten into a five.' To the next farmer, when he appeared, he said, 'And how much do you owe the estate?' 'A thousand bushels of wheat,' came the reply. 'Never mind,' said the factor, 'Take the pen and change the ten into an eight.'

So the accounts were falsified, the books were cooked, as

the saying goes. It is the kind of thing that still happens too often today. And the sequel? The factor duly got his books; but the farmers remembered the favours he had done them. They took him into their houses and saw to it that he did not starve.

That is the story. But the big surprise is still to come. For we read that, when he had finished it, the Master (that is, Jesus) commended the factor for acting wisely. Why did our Lord praise this rogue? Was it for his rascality? Never! He praised him for his realism and resourcefulness in an emergency. 'For,' Christ commented, 'the sons of this world are wiser in their own generation than the sons of light.' In other words, the men who live only for this world – and we have plenty of them today – show far more realism and resource in their business than God's people do in theirs. 'Oh, if only my followers,' Christ is saying, 'would bring a like realism and dedication to the work of God's kingdom!'

And, if we are honest, is not this only too true? Your golfer will spend hours in practising his shots, while your professing Christian can hardly find five minutes to say his daily prayers. Your salesman will become a silver-tongued evangelist for some tuppence ha'penny gadget, while Christ's follower can often hardly say a coherent and convincing word for him whom he calls Lord and Saviour.

Or take some ardent Communist who devotes every waking hour to spreading the gospel according to Karl Marx, never missing a trade-union meeting, never neglecting a chance to sow discontent among his fellow-workers. Can we not hear Christ saying in his parable, 'Here we have a man wholly of this world, with no hope of a blessed hereafter. Yet what zeal he shows! Ah, if only my follower were half as zealous in the work of that church which I died upon a cross to establish!'

But our Lord's point may be illustrated still further. Most people believe in taking out insurance policies. What do such policies signify? Are they not all forms of preparedness for any eventuality in this world?

Then why don't many who call themselves Christians devote to the high business of eternity the same effort they devote to the daily business of time? We Christians profess to believe that 'the grave is not the goal'. Our hope is set on 'a kingdom eternal in the heavens', where Christ now reigns with his Father and all the saints. But are we in fact half as eager to prepare ourselves for a 'room' in what Christ called his 'Father's house' as we are in insuring ourselves against the chances and changes of this world?

'Oh, if only my Christians would show more zeal and devotion!' This is the response Christ asks of each of us. And the odd thing is that, when we make this response, it turns out to be the gateway to a fuller and worthier life in this world, not to mention the world which is to come.

Of course only he who makes the venture will prove that this is true. But, if Christ, speaking through this tale about the rascally factor, can touch one single soul to a new devotion, these words of mine will not have been spoken in vain. He who has ears to hear, let him hear!

13

Grumpy Neighbour and Callous Judge

Luke 11.5-8; 18.2-8

Our Lord Jesus had an unforgettable way of arguing from the human to the divine. He believed human analogies could figure forth to men God's nature and will. For him, human experience was a kind of springboard for the adventure of faith. He had a way of saying, 'Take the very best you know among humans. God is all that – and incomparably more.' So, starting from human values, he invited his disciples to project them into the unseen world and find in them a reflection of the invisible God, Maker of heaven and earth.

Take, for example, his words in the Sermon on the Mount:

> Is there a man among you who will offer his son a stone when he asks for bread, or a snake when he asks for fish? If you then, bad as you are, know how to give your children what is good for them, how much more will your heavenly Father give good things to those who ask him?

So Jesus encouraged his followers to believe in God's goodness. Now, as theology is simply 'faith thinking', so prayer is faith in action. Our Lord never defined prayer; he

48

did better – he gave his disciples a pattern prayer, and in his parables bade them 'expect great things from God'.

Take this story of his about The Grumpy Neighbour (traditionally known as 'The Friend at Midnight'). Late one night a hungry traveller turned up unexpectedly at a friend's house and caught him without a bit of bread in his cupboard. The only thing the householder could do was to knock up a neighbour and ask him for three loaves – the usual meal for one person. And very politely he did, explaining why he had to.

Now peep into the single-roomed house of the sleeping neighbour. His children are bedded in a row on a raised mat, with the parents one at each end, when suddenly at midnight there comes a hammering at the door. The head of the house, startled from his slumbers, is not amused. 'Don't be a confounded nuisance,' he growls to the knocker outside. 'My door was locked hours ago. If I get up, I'll disturb the whole family. No, I'm staying where I am – in bed.'

But our hero, outside in the dark, refuses to take No for an answer. On he keeps knocking until at last in sheer desperation the householder gets up, unbolts the door and hands out the three loaves.

Jesus is talking to his disciples about prayer. 'If a human friend, however unwilling,' he says, 'can be induced to get up and give help, how much more will God your heavenly Father be ready to supply your needs.'

This is what believing prayer is like. The disciple with a faith like this will open his heart freely to his heavenly Father, sure that he will hear him. He will also be able to accept whatever God sends, believing that the All-wise God knows his children's needs better than they do themselves.

Seven chapters later in his Gospel, Luke 'the beloved physician', as Paul names him, has preserved another parable of Jesus about prayer. Traditionally known as 'The Importunate Widow', it would better be called 'The Callous Judge'. The scene is a law-court with the plaintiff a poor widow whose opponent has refused to settle a lawful debt. So daily the woman keeps coming before the judge and crying, 'Give me justice against my oppressor!' But the judge, by his own avowal, is a man who is swayed neither by religious principle nor by public opinion. At first he does nothing. A helpless widow, he thinks, without money or influence – why bother about her? Doubtless, when she started up in court he said, 'Next case, please!' But, if the judge could keep on, so could the widow. Next day she was back again in court, and this went on day after day until at last the judge relented and gave her justice. 'Maybe I don't give a damn for God or man,' we can almost hear him saying, 'yet because this woman keeps pestering me, I will give her justice.' And he did.

The judge, need we say, is not offered as a picture of what God is like. Jesus is not portraying God as some dour ungracious deity who needs to be badgered into compliance. His meaning is: if even this callous judge could be moved to act by that widow's persistence, how much more will God answer his people's prayers for vindication!

What these two stories show, as indeed his whole life shows, is how constantly Jesus leaned on God, believing in the power of prayer, because he knew the kind of being the great 'hearer of prayer' was. And is not our Lord still calling his followers to the same kind of prayer?

To the religious man prayer is something more than, if I may so put it, crying up the chimney of the universe for presents from a celestial Santa Claus. To the religious man it is what original research is to the scientist – by it we make contact with reality, with the last reality in the universe. It is the very life-blood of religion – or if you like, our life-line with the unseen world which lies ever over and above the curtain of our senses. And the sense of God will quickly fade from the heart of a man who gives up praying.

Then why in these dark and troubled times don't we Christians make more use of what has been called, in Milton's phrase, 'the great two-handed engine at our door'?

It was Abraham Lincoln, America's greatest son, who said, 'I have been driven many times to my knees by the overwhelming conviction that I had nowhere else to go. My own wisdom and that of all about me seemed insufficient for the day.' It was Lord Tennyson who wrote:

> More things are wrought by prayer than this world dreams of.

And a greater than Lincoln or Tennyson who assured his disciples, as he still assures us:

> Ask, and it will be given you.
> Seek, and you will find.
> Knock, and it will be opened to you (Matt. 7.7).

So, Christian friends, one and all, keep knocking!

14

The Talents

Matt. 25.14–28

For us, nowadays, a 'talent' denotes some natural gift or aptitude for, let us say, maths or music, acting or athletics. But in the New Testament it means a sum of money. At present-day values, a talent must have been worth about £5000. We have to think, then, of the first servant in the story being given £25,000, the second £10,000, and the third £5000. But the precise amounts do not matter greatly, for the story is about faithfulness rather than finance, and we would do well to re-name it 'Money in Trust'.

A wealthy man (Jesus says), about to go abroad, entrusted three of his servants with the sums already mentioned, expecting them, in his absence, to put them to good use.

On returning from his travels, he proceeded to settle accounts with them. Two servants who had doubled their capital not only were rewarded with their master's 'Well done!', but got big promotions.

But the third servant confessed that, fearing to risk his master's money, he had, for safety's sake, dug a hole and buried his talent in the ground. Now he restored to his master the sum he had received. But if he expected praise, he was rudely undeceived. 'You lazy rascal,' said his master. 'You put me down, didn't you, for a man who drives a hard bargain. You ought to have put my money on deposit in the bank, and I would have got it back now with good interest.'

So the 'lazy rascal' was relieved of the £5000 which was then given to his most enterprising colleague.

That is Christ's story. What is its real point? That we all have a varying endowment of natural gifts, and that if we don't use them, we lose them? This is true, but it is not the original meaning of the parable.

All Christ's parables bore upon a definite historical situation, namely, the coming of God's kingdom or reign. Our Lord saw his ministry as the supreme crisis in God's agelong dealings with his ancient people Israel. And this story is one of several in which he warned Israel and her rulers of the divine judgment overhanging them. (Think of little parables like The Weather Signs and The Man on his Way to Court, as also his prophecy of the Temple's destruction.)

The other thing to note is that this story has three characters in it and that, by the rule of 'end-stress', the spotlight falls on the third one – the 'lazy rascal' who had done nothing with the talent entrusted to him.

For whom does he stand? He stands for the religious rulers of Israel in Christ's day. God had entrusted them with his word – his unique revelation of himself and his will – and they had fallen down on their trust. They had hoarded away that saving knowledge of God and his purpose which should have been 'a light to lighten the Gentiles'. What was meant for all mankind they had kept to themselves. Such hoarding was tantamount to defrauding God of his own, and for this they would have to answer, as in fact they did, only a generation later, when, as Jesus had predicted, Jerusalem and its Temple fell to the advancing legions of Rome.

But (someone will say) all this is ancient history. What relevance has Christ's parable for us today? The answer is not doubtful. The Christian church is the *new* Israel. We stand where old Israel once stood, confronted by the same divine demands. And the question which God puts to us is this: 'What have you done with the spiritual wealth I entrusted to you for all men?'

The gospel is the good news of God's redeeming love in Christ for sinful men and women. Have we been faithful stewards of the spiritual wealth entrusted to us? Have we proclaimed the gospel in all its grandeur, or have we accommodated it to the scepticism and humanism of the day? Have we rung out the good news of 'the old old story' to the 'lost' men and women of our generation, or have we allowed our preoccupation with our own domestic problems to stifle the clear witness which we as Christians ought to be making to a sin-sick and fear-ridden world?

This is the central thrust of Christ's story for us today. It is a rebuke to all slothful and 'safety-first' Christians.

Dr David Read of New York has told us of a fellow-prisoner of his in a POW camp during the last war. Like the other prisoners, he regularly received from home blocks of chocolate. And for the last three months of the war he carefully stored away every slab which he received, only to find, when he unwrapped his parcel, a heap of uneatable mould!

There are Christians like this man, conservators of the worst kind. It is good to preserve 'the faith once for all delivered to the saints'. But it is a bad conservatism which makes Christians hug to themselves the spiritual treasure they have received, and refuse the risks involved in sharing it with others in a world that needs the gospel.

Your wrongly conservative Christian would like, in a dangerous world, to wrap up the gospel and not expose it to what Walter Lipmann called 'the acids of modernity'.

Or perhaps he says, in the old *cliché*, 'charity begins at home'. Therefore let us try to keep Britain Christian rather than indulge in the luxury of foreign missions. So he scurries down the funk hole of a dead orthodoxy on the plea of defending the faith.

On the other hand, your rightly conservative Christian is he who realizes that, if we do not use, we lose. Here, from Christ himself, is a warning which we ignore at our peril. 'Trade till I come' is still our Lord's command to his church today. Let us heed it and obey, lest, like old Israel, we incur the judgment of God.

15

The Man on his Way to Court

Luke 12.57–59

Our Lord was far more interested in politics – not party politics but the politics of his own nation in relation to God's purpose – than many of us have supposed. Consider, for example, the two parables in the twelfth chapter of Luke's Gospel rightly named 'The Weather Signs' and 'The Man on his Way to Court'.[1]

Jesus said to the people, 'When you see cloud banking up in the west, you say at once, "It is going to rain", and rain it does. And when the wind is from the south, you say, "There will be a heat wave", and there is. What hypocrites you are! You know how to interpret the appearance of earth and sky; how is it you cannot interpret this fateful hour?

And why do you not judge for yourselves what is the right course? When you are going with your opponent to court, make an effort to settle with him while you are still on the way; otherwise he may drag you before the judge, and the judge hand you over to the constable, and the constable put you in jail. I tell you, you will not come out till you have paid the last farthing' (NEB).

Let us concentrate on the second story of 'The Man on his Way to Court'.

The insolvent debtor en route for the law-court is old Israel. The 'way to court' is Jesus' way of describing the impending crisis in his nation's history, a crisis which, he says, will bring God's judgment on the nation. Old Israel stands at the crossroads and must decide which way she will go. She must choose whether to align herself with God's purpose embodied in himself or else, pursuing the path of nationalism, enter on a collision course with Rome which must end in ruin.

What makes the decision so urgent is the shortness of the time. If his countrymen were in similar straits financially, they would settle with their creditor long before they reached it. But, alas, in the far greater crisis of their nation, 'eyes have they but they see not'. Could they but realize their peril, they would see that the only right thing to do was to turn back before it was too late and come penitently to God, whose purpose in history goes forward, whether men will or no.

Such was the original meaning of the parable.

The historical crisis which inspired the story is long past. It came to a head a generation later in Israel's fatal clash with mighty Rome. Old Israel fell to Roman arms, Jerusalem was taken, its walls broken down, and its Temple burnt.

But if old Israel, by her disobedience, forfeited her place in God's purpose, out of that crisis was born the new Israel which is the church of Christ.

But, you may say, what has all this ancient history to do with us? And what relevance has the story of 'The Man on his Way to Court' for Christians today?

In every age, crises (and the word 'crisis' literally means 'judgment') of one sort or another confront the church. One came in the sixteenth century with what we call the Reformation. Today South Africa's policy of *apartheid* constitutes another crisis for the church and the world, as we all know. And so on.

With the help of hindsight it is easy for us to condemn old Israel's blindness in her 'fateful hour'. But has the new Israel, i.e. the church, never been blind to the 'signs of the times' and failed to interpret God's action in history?

Think back to the years before 1914. When the crisis of the Great World War broke on the world, were there not many Christians who found their faith sadly unsettled by that catastrophe? How could there be a good God, they said, if he permitted such suffering and horror to happen? If they had read the signs of the times with truly Christian eyes, how differently they might have construed the catastrophe! They might have seen that with such a Europe, with such a neglect of God and his righteousness, the wonder, the disquieting thing, would have been if no divine judgment had fallen on our materialistic civilization and our degenerate Christianity.

Since then we have had a second World War. But have we yet learned the lessons God teaches us in the crises of history and interpreted them in the light of his nature and purpose as revealed in Christ?

It is a question worth serious pondering, for since our scientists have learnt how to split the atom, the issues have grown immeasurably graver. May we not see in the invention of the atomic bomb 'God's awful warning' to modern man of his potential to destroy himself and the world as we know it? Is not our civilization now in the position of the debtor in Christ's parable? If we persist in the politics of blatant self-interest and 'devil take the hindmost'; if we fail to heal the open sores of humanity – racialism, antisemitism, world hunger and the rest; if we do not resolutely attack the problems which cause nation to war against nation; and if the statesmen of the world do not come together and for ever ban the stockpiling of atomic missiles, will not mankind be in peril of 'paying the last farthing' in nuclear holocaust?

This is surely the biggest crisis now facing humanity, and the church, in its prophetic role, ought to be facing men with the dread issues, saying to this generation as Christ said to his: 'You know how to interpret the appearance of earth and sky; but why do you not know how to interpret the signs of the present time?'

'He who has ears to hear, let him hear!'

16

Dives and Lazarus

Luke 16.19-31

What do you make of Jesus' story about Dives and Lazarus, or, more simply, Rich Man, Poor Man?

Some have supposed that in it he was giving us a preview of the next world. Others have thought he was answering the question, 'Is there another chance in the next life for those who have failed in this one?' Both views are mistaken. All the story tells us about the after-life is that there *is* one and that our conduct here affects our destiny there. As for the background scenery – Abraham's bosom (a Jewish phrase for the abode of the blessed after death), paradise and hell – our Lord is simply adopting the popular images of the time as a setting for the truth he has to teach.

What we have in the parable is a little drama in two acts, plus an epilogue.

In Act I the scene is the visible world. Here is Dives decked out in 'purple and fine linen' (shall we say, in his Savile Row suitings) and 'feasting sumptuously every day' (shall we say, eating his caviare and drinking his gin and tonic). Then, side by side, we are shown Lazarus in his rags at the rich man's gate, his body full of ulcers which the street dogs rasp with their tongues, while he only keeps himself alive by eating the bits of bread which the rich man's guests wipe their fingers on before throwing them away. Dives in his luxury and finery, Lazarus in his rags and sores – this is the picture.

But when the curtain rises on Act II, the visible world has given place to the invisible one, and there has been a dramatic change in the two men's fortunes. Before us now appear heaven and hell on one small stage. But now Lazarus reclines on Abraham's bosom at the heavenly banquet, while Dives is in hell, racked by thirst and tormented in flame.

Moreover, though in life Dives had never spared a glance for the beggar at his gate, now he sees him – afar off and in felicity – and would fain make him his friend. So he appeals to Father Abraham for help from Lazarus, only to be told that it is too late. 'Dives,' he is told, 'You got your good things in life, while Lazarus got the ills. Now the fortunes are reversed.' 'Besides, between us and you there is a great gulf fixed.' In other words, God has made his judgment on your lives, and against his judgment there is no appeal.

If the tale had ended there, its meaning would surely have been: 'The inhuman man is a lost soul. He goes into eternity without a single friend.' But the conversation continues and takes a different turn in what we have named the Epilogue.

In it Dives asked Abraham to send Lazarus back to earth in order to warn his five brothers lest a similar fate befall them. To understand this, we may imagine the men who heard Jesus' story objecting, 'That is final all right, but is it fair? If Dives had known what a roasting he was in for hereafter, how differently he would have treated Lazarus on earth!'

To this objection Jesus, speaking through the mouth of Abraham, replies: 'They have Moses and the Prophets; let them listen to them.' In other words, in the Bible they already have a sufficient guide on how they ought to live, and they need no more. But this does not satisfy Dives. 'Ah, but,' he says, 'if only someone would go back from the dead, and warn them, they would mend their ways.' Once again Jesus dismisses the objection: 'If they do not listen to Moses and the Prophets, they will pay no heed, even if someone should rise from the dead.'

That is Christ's story. What is its meaning for us today?

First, and plainly, it is a lesson in humanity or, better, humaneness. In it we catch echoes of the same voice which said in his story of the Last Judgment, 'Inasmuch as you did it to one of the least of these my brethren, you did it to me . . .' God meets us at our own door, and his question is, 'What have you done with Lazarus?' As we claim to be Christ's followers today, we are called to do what we can to feed the hungry, clothe the naked, and help the helpless. For to perform such acts of love is, in Christ's own phrase, 'to lay up treasure in heaven'.

The other lesson comes in what we have named the Epilogue. This parable, scholars agree, was aimed at the Sadducees, the rich materialists of the day, who lived only for the day and had no belief in an after-life. Challenged by Jesus, they had replied that they might believe in one, if he would give them some supernatural sign to prove it. Jesus refused. 'Men,' he told them in effect, 'are expected to respond to the revelation of God's truth they now have. If they cannot respond to this, they are unlikely to respond to some more unusual manifestation.' Or, to quote his own words, 'If they won't listen to Moses and the Prophets, they will not be convinced if someone should come back from the dead.'

Today we still have men like these old Sadducees. To all such Jesus says, 'If men with God's revelation before them in the scriptures and poor men lying in misery on their doorsteps, cannot be humane, nothing – neither a revenant from the other world nor a vision of the horrors of hell – will teach them otherwise.'

In short, to the inhuman person the next world will never be more than a subject for unanswered questions. But for those who try to love and show compassion to all the unfortunates, as Christ has bidden us, it will be what it was for him – another part of his Father's House, and as real as that which we now see.

17

The Grain of Wheat
John 12.24

The parables about The Sower and The Seed Growing Secretly were spoken in Galilee long before the shadow of a cross began to lengthen across the path of Jesus. But to the imagery of the sown seed and the harvest he was to come back in Jerusalem in the last days of his earthly ministry.

St John sets the parable of The Grain of Wheat just before the third and last Passover of Jesus' ministry. It was evoked, he says, by the desire of some Greeks to 'interview' Jesus. For Jesus, this desire was the signal that a new and wider phase in his mission – a ministry to the Gentiles – was at hand. 'The hour has come,' he cried, 'for the Son of Man to be glorified.' But he also said, almost in the same breath, 'Now is my soul troubled.' Why? One suggestion is that at this point the devil made a final attempt to divert him from his God-appointed destiny. Why not abandon Jerusalem and his stiff-necked fellow-countrymen and betake himself to the bigger world of the Gentiles? This temptation Jesus put behind him. There could be no evasion of the Cross. So, prefacing it with a doubled Amen, Jesus uttered the parable of The Grain of Wheat: 'Truly, truly I tell you, unless a grain of wheat falls into the earth and dies, it remains alone; but if it dies, it bears much fruit.'

Some have taken Jesus to be laying down a grim law of all human life:

> And all through life I see a cross
> Where sons of God give up their breath,
> There is no gain except by loss,
> There is no life except by death.

Yet, so to generalize this parable's meaning is to forget that it was uttered almost in the shadow of the Cross. As in his saying about the Ransom for Many (Mark 10.45), Jesus is thinking of the necessity and purpose of his death. He is foretelling the rich redemptive harvest which his completed Passion will bring with it.

Once earlier, and with a noble impatience, he had cried, 'I have come to send fire on the earth, and how I wish it were already kindled! But I have a baptism to undergo, and how constricted I am until the ordeal is over!' Before the fire of the gospel can blaze, the bearer of the gospel must die. His baptism in blood is his necessary initiation into a fuller and freer activity where he 'will be let loose in the world where neither Roman nor Jew can stop his truth'.

This, though the metaphor is different, is essentially what Jesus is saying in his parable about The Grain of Wheat. His death is the inescapable condition of his ministry becoming greatly fruitful in the wider world. If it is to yield its rich crop, the planted seed must be watered by the bloody sweat of his Passion.

Nearly three centuries before Christ, the great Greek scientist Archimedes had said, 'Give me a proper place to stand on, and I will move the world.' 'Give me a Cross to hang on', said Jesus, 'and I will draw all men to myself' (John 12.32).

Has not our Lord's prescience been vindicated? 'The Cross of Christ,' wrote Mrs Hamilton King, 'is more to us than all his miracles.' 'Christ died on the Tree,' Thomas Carlyle told Emerson, as they walked the Galloway moors together, 'that built Dunscore Kirk yonder.' 'In the Cross of Christ I glory, towering o'er the wrecks of time,' wrote Sir John Bowring.

But if the parable concerns the necessity and purpose of Christ's death, his saying which follows it carries its corollary for every true follower of his: 'The man who loves himself is lost.' Here was something new. 'In all Greek thought,' wrote William Temple, 'there is no appreciation of the excellence of self-sacrifice. This is the point – the vital point – where the ethics of the Gospel leave the ethics of Greek philosophy far behind.'

Self-sacrifice, says our Lord, is the way to self-fulfilment. Your true Christian dies to live. This, as Paul and all the great saints have known, is a law of the Christian life at its deepest and best. And the blood of the martyrs, from Stephen to Dietrich Bonhoeffer, is ever the seed of church.

18

The Owner's Son

Mark 12.1-9 NEB

This parable, traditionally known as 'The Wicked Husband-men', but which we propose to rename 'The Owner's Son', is possibly the last Jesus ever told. Our Lord has ridden in meek majesty into Jerusalem and cleansed the Temple, thus setting in train the whole series of events destined to issue in the fall of Jerusalem and the rise of the new Israel. Now in the holy city the rulers of Jewry have resolved to make an end of this messianic pretender; the skies are louring; and Calvary is not far away.

It is to these rulers that Jesus tells the story which is half parable, half allegory. Some of its words recall Isaiah's Song of the Vineyard (Isa. 5.1-7), where the prophet had likened Israel to God's vineyard which had not yielded its proper fruit and was ripe for judgment. But, if some of the words in the story are old, the application is new and startling.

A man, says Jesus, planted a vineyard, and when he had put it in order, let it out to some tenants before he went abroad. (Absentee landlords were common, then as now.) Before he went, he made a bargain with his tenants on a crop-sharing basis: at vintage time they were to pay him as rent part of the produce. So, when the season came, he sent one of his servants to collect it. But an absentee landlord is fair game for unscrupulous tenants. They paid the servant

67

– with blows. A second servant whom he sent they outraged; and a third they slew. And so on.

Desperate situations require daring remedies. The owner now conceived a bold idea. 'They have treated my servants thus,' he said to himself, 'but if I send my own son, they must respect him.' But the tenants were wickeder than he imagined. When the son appeared, they whispered to each other, 'This is the heir. If we get rid of him, the property will be ours.' So they killed him, cast his body outside the vineyard, and seized the property.

'What do you think the owner of the vineyard will do?' said Jesus as he ended his tale. 'He will come and give the vineyard to others.'

In Palestine then they had economic crises as we have them now, and in the agrarian discontent of the time it might have been just a typical story of what befell an absentee landlord's property. But it wasn't. *Gulliver's Travels* is now a young people's classic; but how many of our children who now read it realize that Dean Swift, its author, meant it as a savage satire on his own contemporaries?

So too is Jesus' story. For the vineyard is Israel, the people whom God had chosen to be the special recipients of his grace, that they in turn might share it with the whole world. The tenants are the rulers of Israel down the centuries. The servants are the long line of prophets, or spokesmen for God, from Elijah to John the Baptist. And the only son and heir is Christ himself.

The parable, then, is our Lord's picture of Israel's history. Thus and thus did God deal with his chosen people, and thus and thus have they treated his messengers. 'O Jerusalem, Jerusalem, who killest the prophets,' Jesus had said (Luke 13.34). And now events were moving to their awful climax.

So it was not a story in which all the characters were fictitious. It was in fact autobiography. For the man who told it was its central figure, and very soon the tale came fully true. God sent his only Son to his people, making his last appeal, and they spiked him to a cross, outside the northern wall of Jerusalem.

All this is an old story now; but we cannot dismiss it by saying that it is about some first-century Jews and no concern of ours. We belong to the new Israel which is the Christian church, and if the church has inherited old Israel's place, it inherits also the danger of God's judgment. Let us consider the point more fully.

The Jews killed the owner's son, but they did not end his life. On the third day, by God's power, he rose from the dead. They but released him for wider and fuller work. What Caiaphas, Pilate and the others were trying to do on the first Good Friday was to stop the ministry of Jesus. But, if there is one thing quite certain, it is that the ministry of Jesus went on. It still goes on today. No longer is the owner's son confined within the little land of Palestine. Through the Holy Spirit's work, he has become the living Lord of more than a thousand million people. Moreover, God's vineyard is now co-terminous with the globe itself. Its tenants are no longer the Jews, but men and women of practically every race under the sun. And to us in this twentieth century the parable comes with its Word of God.

First, it speaks in judgment. We are God's tenants. To us, as to old Israel, God looks for the fruits of faith and love and obedience. Of us he requires that we 'do justly, love mercy, and walk humbly with our God'. Dare we say that we are producing these fruits?

True, today there is an *ecclēsia*, a church which is world-wide. The mustard seed has grown into a great tree in whose branches the wild birds have come to roost. But, alas, there is another and darker side to the picture. Still, as in Christ's day, 'the great ones of the Gentiles' lord it over their weaker brethren. White men oppress their black brothers. Still this earth, which is the Lord's and 'might be fair and free', they parcel out as if it were their own. And as our vision ranges over the world, we see how many places in God's vineyard men have turned into armed camps from which they menace each other with weapons of destruction, with the atomic bomb as 'God's awful warning to mankind'.[1]

Nor is it hard to hear Christ's last parable speaking to us in challenge. 'Having yet therefore one son, his well-beloved, he sent him last.' Christ is God's last appeal, his final challenge, to us rebellious men. 'Here in my Son,' says the Almighty Father, 'I have shown you all my heart – revealed my deepest purposes of mercy and love. Will you not turn and heed him and obey?'

Finally, the parable speaks to us in hope. 'They will reverence my son.' And, be it soon or be it late, in the end men will. For Christ is the heir of all that God has made and is yet to come into his own. As St Paul put it, God's purpose is that men shall become 'joint-heirs' with Christ, 'the eldest among a large family of brothers' (Rom. 8.29). For the present men may make havoc of God's vineyard, but they will not do so for ever. For, unless the gospel is one gigantic fiction, we look for a time when he who now reigns at God's right hand will openly come into his full inheritance, and the Lord of the vineyard will hold a final accounting. Happy the man who on that day will be adjudged a faithful tenant in his master's vineyard!

19

The Ten Bridesmaids

Matt. 25.1–12

Here we have a story from real life in first-century Palestine – its details true to life even today – about ten village girls on their way to a wedding, five of whom skimped their preparations and lived to rue their carelessness.

In the parable the ten girls, friends of the bride, planned to go out and meet the bridegroom when he came with his friends to conduct the bride to his house for the wedding. Their role was to provide a lighted escort for the bridegroom's party. But, as sometimes happens at weddings, there was a hitch. All ten bridesmaids appeared with lighted torches; but only five remembered to bring oil in flasks to replenish them, if the bridegroom should be delayed.

As in fact he was, so that, wearied with waiting, the ten girls dozed off to sleep, and it was midnight before the shout went up, 'The bridegroom's on his way!' It was then that five of the girls found their torches going out for lack of oil. So they sought to borrow from the other five, only to be told, 'No, there won't be enough for us all. You had better go to the shop and buy some for yourselves.' So off went the foolish five in quest of oil.

Alas, they were not long gone when the bridegroom did arrive, and the five wise girls went off with him and his friends to the wedding. Later, when the five foolish ones turned up breathlessly, they found the reception door shut in their faces. 'Let us in! Let us in!' they begged. But all they got from the bridegroom was a dusty answer, as if to say, 'If you can't turn up in time, you don't deserve to be here.'

'And the door was shut.' What a grim ending to what should have been a happy story! Why did Jesus tell it?

The answer is that this is one of several parables in which Jesus warned his hearers that the supreme crisis in God's dealings with his chosen people was approaching, that the Messiah was coming to the very home and heart of Jewry, and that the issue for them could only be disaster if, like the foolish girls in the story, they were found unready.

It is matter of history that old Israel was caught unprepared. When God sent his Son the Messiah among them, they were both unready and unrecipient. 'He came to his own home,' said St John sadly, 'and his own people did not receive him' (John 1.11). But out of that crisis there was born a new Israel, the Christian church. If that church looked back to the cross and the resurrection, they also 'spoke to each other softly of a hope' when Christ would come again in glory, as they prayed, *Marana tha!*, which means 'Come, O Lord!' (I Cor. 16.22); and, naturally enough, they reapplied Christ's story about The Ten Bridesmaids to their own situation, seeking to prepare their members for the great day.

Today, like them, we still stand 'between the times', between Christ's first and second comings. He himself did not know the time of his coming in glory (Mark 13.32). No more do we, and it is foolish to speculate on what is a reserved secret in the breast of God. Yet this does not lessen the need for Christians to be prepared.

Writing on this matter Professor C. F. D. Moule has well said:

New Testament thought on the Last Things, at its deepest and best, always concentrates on what God has already done for men in Christ. It does not say, How long will it be before the final whistle blows full time? Rather it says, Where ought I to be to receive the next pass? What really matters is that the kick-off has already taken place, the game is on, and we have a captain to lead us to victory.[1]

Is not this a modern way of expressing the summons to Christian preparedness? We know him whom we shall meet when the human race reaches its last frontier post and comes face to face with God in Christ.[2] Christ is both our captain now who, unseen but not unknown, leads us on to victory, and the one who will be revealed in glory at the last day (Col. 3.4).

The parable, then, is a call to Christian readiness like that in Philip Doddridge's hymn:

> Let all your lamps be bright,
>   And trim the golden frame,
> Gird up your loins, as in his sight,
>   For awesome is his name.
>
> O happy servant he
>   In such a posture found,
> He shall his Lord with rapture see,
>   And be with honour crowned.
>
> Christ shall the banquet spread
>   With his own royal hand,
> And raise that faithful servant's head
>   Amid the angelic band.

20

The Last Judgment

Matt. 25.31-46

'You seem, sir,' said an Oxford lady to Doctor Samuel
Johnson in one of his despondent hours when the fear of
death and judgment lay heavy upon him, 'to forget the
merits of our Redeemer.' 'Madame,' replied the honest old
man, 'I do not forget the merits of my Redeemer; but my
Redeemer has said that he will set some on his right hand
and some on his left.' What haunted Johnson's mind was
Christ's parable of The Last Judgment, sometimes called the
story of The Sheep and the Goats.

Nowadays a psychiatrist would doubtless dismiss Johnson
as a religious neurotic. Modern man, we are told, isn't
bothering about his sins. We live in a 'permissive age' when
men would fain forget that they are finally accountable to
God for what they do, or fail to do, in this life. For them,
moral distinctions have become blurred; sins appear as
aimable weaknesses; and they tend to shuffle out of responsi-
bility for the evil deeds they do. Small wonder that modern
man no longer shares Johnson's fears about death and
judgment.

Yet, if we believe in a living and righteous God, holding
that we are responsible to him for what we do, or fail to do,
in this life, we cannot thus lightly dismiss Christ's teaching.
No doubt our pious forefathers to whom 'the great white

throne' was a solemnizing certainty, depicted the Great Assize in ways no longer credible by us today. Yet no creed can be called Christian which does not include a reference to what Addison called 'that great Day when we shall all of us be contemporaries and make our appearance together'.

So to Christ's parable about it. 'When the Son of man comes in his glory,' it begins, 'he will sit in state on his throne, with all the nations gathered before him.' Here 'the Son of man', who later in the story is called 'the King', can only be Christ himself, as 'all the nations' must mean 'all the Gentiles'. In the parable, therefore, we have our Lord's reply to the question, 'By what criterion will those be judged who have never known you in the flesh?' His answer is: 'These men have met me in my brethren, for all God's needy children are my brothers. Therefore on the great Day they will be judged by the compassion they have shown to all poor and afflicted folk in whom they have met me in disguise, and, if they have fulfilled the royal law of love, they will share in my Father's heavenly kingdom.'

'Inasmuch as you did it to one of the least of these my brothers,' says our Lord, 'you did it unto me.' Such is Christ's solidarity with all God's sad and suffering children that to show love to them is show love to himself. In other words, on the great Day, the justification (or acquittal) of those who have never known Christ will be a justification not by faith but by *love*. And if for others there is condemnation, by the same token it will be for lack of love to such persons in their misery.

Our parable has been called 'the story of the great surprises': on the one hand, the unfeigned surprise of 'the blessed ones' who had, so to speak, stumbled into paradise, all unaware that in helping the needy they had been confronting Christ himself; and, on the other hand, the pained surprise of the condemned who would, they implied, have acted so very differently if only they had known that those wretched and unfriended people were Christ's brothers.

The parable then would seem to have been Christ's answer to a question about the judgment in store for the Gentiles. But does it not still carry its message for us today? Through it our Lord says to us, 'The grievous sins are those of inhumanity, of callous unconcern for the sad, the hungry, the stranger and the prisoner.'

For us, then, the parable should be a summons to become Christ's 'soldiers of pity' to all the sad and suffering folk who meet us on life's road and in whom he himself confronts us incognito. Still today he says to us, 'Inasmuch as you have done it to one of the least of these my brothers, you have done it unto me.'

> He that careth for a wounded brother
> Watcheth not alone.
> There are three in the darkness together.
> And the third is the Lord.

Happy are those who thus find Christ, for theirs is the kingdom of heaven.

21

The Two Builders

Matt. 7.24-27

What Christ takes for granted is always significant. And what he takes for granted in his parable of The Two Builders which closes the Sermon on the Mount, is that the life of his followers will inevitably contain an element of storm and stress. Later, in the Upper Room before going out to the Cross, he explicitly told his disciples, as he had told them before in his Beatitudes, 'In the world you will have trouble' (John 16.33). This being so, it matters supremely whether we build the house of our life upon rock or upon sand.

The story of The Two Builders is yet another story from real life. Jesus may well have seen with his own eyes a sand-based house begin to shake and shudder when the gales blew and the floods rose. How vividly he describes it! 'Down came the rain, down swept the spate, heavily the winds blew,' till we reach the climax: 'Down it fell with a great crash!'

The contrast in the parable is between a 'prudent' man who took care to found his house on rock deep-hidden below the dry water-course, and a 'stupid' man who built his on the smooth sand of the torrent bed. The outcome was predictable: when the great rains of autumn fell and the water-course became a raging river, one house stood firm, the other collapsed like a house of cards.

The wisdom of founding on rock, the folly of founding on sand, is the point of the parable. The rock-built house stands for hearing *and* doing what Christ says; the sand-built house for hearing it only. And the storm is any time of severe testing in this earthly life of ours. In such a crisis the secret of security will be a life built on the person and teaching of our Lord.

'Hearing *and* doing' is what matters. One of the saddest words Christ ever uttered was: 'Why do you call me Lord, Lord, and do not the things I say?' (Luke 6.46). So it was with his first followers. Though they were quick to applaud his words, they were soon found wanting when it came to acting on them. And down nineteen Christian centuries the problem has ever been the gap between profession and practice.

Happily in modern times we have seen in the church a new and welcome emphasis on what is called 'Christian Action' – the realization that, as St James said, 'faith without works is dead', the conviction that, if our Christian witness to the world is to be effective, it must incarnate itself in deeds of compassion to the poor, the hungry, the disinherited and the oppressed. And we must hope and pray that this call to Christian Action will be heard ever more widely in the coming years.

But in this parable Jesus is not just saying that profession which does not issue in practice were better suppressed altogether. He is saying, 'It is a question of *my* way – which is God's way – or disaster!' Listen: 'Everyone who hears these words of mine and acts on them . . .' Jesus stands before men and tells them that he has laid down principles of action which they neglect at their peril. Only one who was conscious that his will was completely synonymous with the divine will could have spoken thus. And what he says is: 'My way – or disaster.'

Nor is there any 'alibi' for us here. We cannot plead that we do not know Christ's way, which is God's way. In the Sermon on the Mount and elsewhere he has told us what kind of people we ought to be. And, as the late Dr Joad once said, 'Most of us know that Christ's prescription for good living is the right one.'

Yes, but the prescriber himself goes further: 'Either you act on my prescription,' he says, 'or you court disaster.'

Is not the present state of the world the clearest evidence that Christ is right? 'What shape is the world, Daddy?' said one modern young man to his father. 'The hell of a shape, sonny,' came the reply. What is being assailed today is not merely what John Bunyan called Mansoul, but man's civilization itself. When men despise the divine gentleness of Christ's Beatitudes, when they esteem grabbing better than giving, when for 'the Golden Rule' they substitute the rule of the jungle, there can be only one outcome – disaster.

God is not mocked. Men must abide the consequences of their ungodly actions. This is what the New Testament means by 'the wrath of God' – the antagonism of his holy will to the sin of man. And there is abundant evidence that it is working here and now in this world of ours. Indeed, if God did not so react against human wickedness, we could never be sure that the world was in righteous hands.

Yet, if the parable utters its warning to the whole human race, 'My way, which is God's way – or disaster!', it speaks yet more pointedly to us who belong to 'the household of faith' – the church. What it says to us is: 'Sand – or rock?' Are you content to be merely nominal Christians paying lip-service to Christ and his truth, or are you really on the

Lord's side in the day of the ordeal and resolved to shape your lives by him?

If you decide to make the wise choice – to build your life on rock and not sand – Christ gives you no guarantee that the storms will abate. They may even get worse. What he does promise you is that, even if the world is reeling about you, you have the assurance that your house will stand firm because it it built on solid rock, the granite of God himself.

'When your feet are on the rock,' said Dr David S. Cairns of Aberdeen during the Second World War, 'you can exult even in the whirlpool.' I call that a great Christian saying.

For the Christian God, the Father of Christ – of him 'whose work was done when by his death he took our sins away' – the Father who took Christ out of the grave and 'gave him glory that our faith and hope might be in him' – this God has the evil of the world, even such a one as ours, in the hollow of his hand, as his final triumph over all the works of the devil is assured.

If you and I believe this – and it is the teaching of the New Testament – we are called to go forth into this sinful world and do God's will, knowing not only that we are building upon the Rock of Ages but that, as St Paul said, nothing in this world or out of it will be able to separate us from the love of God revealed in Jesus Christ our Lord.

Rock or sand? On which are *you* building *your* life?

NOTES

NOTES

Chapter 1

1. Above all, C. H. Dodd in his *Parables of the Kingdom*, Hodder 1935.

Chapter 3

1. The statistics are taken from MARCO, an American Missionary Research body.

Chapter 12

1. 'Factor' is the Scots word for a land-steward (Greek *oikonomos*). Dr Moffatt used the word in his well-known translation of the New Testament. In English we might call him 'The Bent Bailiff'.

Chapter 15

1. To these two parables might be added that of The Traveller at Sunset in John's Gospel (John 12.35f.).

Chapter 18

1. So, at its invention, it was described by Principal David S. Cairns of Aberdeen.

Chapter 19

1. *The Birth of the New Testament*, A. & C. Black 1966, 101f.
2. On this whole subject see C. H. Dodd's profound little book, *The Coming of Christ*, Hodder 1951. Nothing better has been written this century on its central theme – Christ's coming, going and return. When Karl Barth read it, he said: 'These are exactly my own views on the matter.'

NOTES